Blurb

Summer Knowles

BookLeaf Publishing

India | USA | UK

Presentation by *BookLeaf Publishing*

Web: www.bookleafpub.com

E-mail: info@bookleafpub.com

ISBN: 9789357446099

First edition 2022

ACKNOWLEDGE MENT

Thank you, dear reader, for enjoying my book.
Thanks mom for encouraging me to write it.

Growing Up

My life is haunted
By a foe that never slows.
Time is relentless.

I don't know what I
want to do, but I can't play
dolls like I used to

somebody tell me
how my life plays out- or give
me a telescope

I just want to know
my future is as bright as
it was years ago.

Predictable, I was.
Was I? Is anyone really?

Summerland

A ring light of sun encircles your curls
Finally, a halo to harmonize with your cherubic
pink lemonade cheeks
White fluffball basking in it with more dignity
than an Egyptian sphinx
Step up to the spindle-shanked trees to see how
tall you've grown!
Bend down to greet a baby frog, metallic spider,
or alien yellow mushroom
Catch a moth but call it dead. Life is wings
a-broken, mysterious baby birds with missing
souls
Trying to change the world, but efforts wear
your skin down more than UV rays
You miss socializing, though you never had
friends. Make several online, but your ties need
a cleanse
Miss independence, you pretend.
New bedroom, adult birthday, quarantine. You
were almost swallowed
by that pint-size picture- taker but it's frac
tured frailty now.
Smile bright, no need to rush your blooming

Broken Nursery

No light. I wait. I gaze. The sky is maimed.
To jump, the cow, I know, they spin! A lie
To flame your nimble heart and stalks now slain.
No turning back the clock when time's awry

No hiding! Suns and moons collide, to speak
Eclipse excites my goose; her egg descends
So what? No gold?! You shriek (and kick my
knee)
I fume. I snort but   breathe   must keep a
friend.

Did Ma tell roosters crowing loud to flee?
No clue. The dish, The spoon. Divorced. You
muse
My voice deflates   I wander hurt at sea
Your words can burn the giants shooing blues

Is marriage dreamy? Cotton seams. A pill
ow. 'member Jack? No crown. The end?
Downhill.

Difficult Postulates of Euclid's Book

I feel
I am
Infinite.
Space, time,
littering losses locked inside little lines.
I remember learning about lines.
I remember using a straightedge to get them ever
so… perfect.
A ruler to rule the beginning, middle, and-
I remember putting the arrows on the ends, just
to notate the fact that they
Never end
I don't remember ever comprehending how lines
could be never ending.
I don't remember getting to plot the points that
didn't land on the line's one-dimensional plane.
Or questioning the dimension's frame.
Am I getting the right angle?
I feel
I am
Erroneous.

In a world of angles, lines, and shapes. Am I a
spectrum of squiggles amongst squares? A
dodecahedron in a dollop of diamonds?
What am I?
Why?
Maybe I'm a circle.
The roundness can't be incoherent, can it?
Unless I'm outside the rendering, the way
aristotle... planned it?
Am I mine to create? Or must I wait…
Until a rotary compass settles on my fate.

malnourished

Death, grief, loss everywhere I go
Facing an appetency-
For what, I don't know

I'm hankering for an anodyne,
Begging for normalcy to feel "fine"
But death is just a meal they're saying,
One we all must learn to swallow.

Survive Survive Survive... thrive. Living,
a Conglomeration of Surviving
and predominantly
Thriving.
We wake up in the earth's soil,
clothing, moss,
Hungering for ambrosia,
to relish the silent feast in the forest.
We look to where the light stands,
Open mouths watering,
Seeking after
nectarous sustenance,
But falling before seizing...

Anything

Foraging for mulberries,
Running, scraped knees,
Blood, welts from trees,
Seeping, icy river
Water through my unclean fingers
Intermingling
With a corrosive stream
Of tears and clots of Red.

Thirsting
Heart spurting
Hands hurting
From holding loss
Lost in thoughts of
Rotting soft
In milkweed floss.
Appetite =ill-defined.

Exo Adaptation

As the snail retreats into its hard shell,
And protects itself from life's sharpest blows,
I so envy its exoskeleton.

Mother Nature, hear me out now. Please.
I demand the armor you fashioned for
the animals of this senseless Earth.
Why engage in a world that hurts and hates?
Why not withdraw into a safety net,
Only soaking up sunlight when needed?

Midnight Mischief

I'm crawling on the ground
When I hear a sound
I rise to my feet,
Hoping no one is around

the whole cake gets snarfed down
At some point, i pass out
Mother finds me...
"It was full of vodka," she says with a frown

Never Noticed

You never noticed that you murdered me.
You never noticed because you never used a
gun,
Never tried a bomb,
Never picked up a knife,
Never threw a grenade,
Nor did you ever, ever assault me.
You never noticed how
the venomous words rolling off your forked
tongue
sent a paralyzing poison into my bloodstream,
and all of your fraudulent facticities
pierced a sword through my heart.

Every wicked betrayal scorched my soul,
While every kiss left me gasping for air.
You tied a noose around my innocence,
And eventually decapitated my ability to ever
love anyone again.
You never noticed that my heart no longer beat
for you.
You never noticed that I possessed a heart, to
begin with.

Time

One of these days, I will find a way to
Bring the granular sands of time to a
Complete halt! No more rushing to retrieve
The minuscule moments Father Time dared
To thieve while you were slaving all day long.

Although, if you look more closely, slaving
can be clearly defined as slumbering.

I suppose... without time, you'd waste your life,
so, perhaps, your bondage ought to remain.

An Eth(n)ical Dilemma Pt 1

Dorothy West thought "To know how much there is to know is the beginning of learning to live." But it's painfully ironic to say live as I think of those of us who've died (and continue to die unjustly). Racism is eternally fatal. Am I strong enough to tackle it head on? What could I possibly say or do, when my idee fixes aren't new? When no one before me has succeeded? I'm disgruntled by my being stumped because my mind continues to galumph and clump. It refuses to think there is no hope or answer. It refuses to still, so it viciously scampers.
I know this dilemma is not unique to my time, yet I feel such a stirring to seize it and call it mine. This stirring surges and urges me to serve my purpose.
To help curb the melancholia inside the ones currently hurting. The forgotten souls, the ones that sit listless, unlistened and unlisted in pits without provisions. Not by their own choice, of course, but by a fate overruled by powers perversely lacking remorse. Alice

Walker wrote, "Healing begins where the wound
was made". But guess what?
After all these years, the "wound" has barely
been found. How could I help us heal?
Inequality is an incapacitating ailment,
whenever I inhale it, but know not what to do to
conclusively impale it.

An Eth(n)ical Dilemma Pt 2

Achebe proclaimed, "The writer cannot expect to be excused from the task of reeducation and regeneration that must be done. In fact, he should march right in front." I won't deny it, there's no way to quiet, the poem, the lyrics, beginning to riot.
I am riled up! I am wrathful! I picked up my pencil to illume my people's anguish, so it can rattle the uncomfortable people who avoid the pits and reek of "ignorance's bliss".

 Honestly? I've allowed ignorance to turn me from the truth. I wore my cultural bias about my own people like my mother wearing a fur coat in winter. Without grasping our history, I detested our pursuit of life, thinking it reprehensible, no-criminal. But now, I am realizing none of us could be at fault because we've always been powerless. We didn't come here by choice, didn't devolve here by choice. In empathizing with my kin now, I see we're all misplaced and diluted. We're all lost with no way home, no way to be included.

If you start with our unjust displacement, then
follow history's most ungracious timeline, you
can slowly piece together... everything. Every
inapt misgiving of today- unemployment, poor
education, incarcerations, crime, police
dehumanizing- can be traced back to slavery. So
maybe clear the USA's webpage history, then
click "restart". Or reboot the country entirely
like Hollywood would. You could backspace

 racism, delete Trump, insert another minority
president after Obama (female preferably).
Then, copy/paste a fair judicial system, equal
wages and class statuses, {This all started with a
prideful mind, so you'd have to re-align the
characters on the page (nothing "centered") and
so on...} That would be my Dream for society
today. After all, you can't ever expect a happily
ever after when you regard the lynching,
segregation, bombings... and the Constitution!
The Founding Fathers didn't even believe we
were fully human, homo sapiens. But in 2020,
many citizens finally possess the sapience to
recognize reality- we were human beings all
along, we've been Americans all along. And our
lives matter.
Thus, I take hold of my blackness. It's not
something I can erase. But also something I
wouldn't replace, it makes me courageous in

every space. It is what I make it, which is why I won't shy away. I can't say I know me or all my history, but I will keep discovering more each day. They will NOT make me

ashamed, will NOT fill me with disdain for my people, tethered by torment and memories of misery, will NOT make me break down or give up, like my ancestors, I will boldly fight to make a brighter future for us; my children will inherit light.

the truth is

I don't have time to waste on pitying me.
I don't have time to waste
  don't have time
      time
          waste
              pity

6 AM

with cheeks water-lily pink
and revved-up for racing feet,
you shove open the back door

in the dewy grass, little brother rolls over you,
brown curls messy and flopping
squawking ducks side-eye you for disturbing
them
finally, breathless,
you both watch the sunrise

Another Day

9/19/20

days and days and-
why does month after month spin me gray?

energy spent.
heart is creaking,
in need of

cradling

nobody talks by not talking anymore

nobody cries
nobody lives   or listens
to what's waving right in front of them

First Kiss

my face is burning.
Why not me?

I wish you'd asked for a dare, but instead, you
said, "truth!"
so she asked you, "Have you had your..." she
paused. Not a one of us moved. "First kiss?"

You nodded, barely holding back a grin. We
weren't even 12 years old yet! my ears were
boiling hot and I bit my tongue after
congratulating you. I was impressed, but also
envious of the one who'd gotten to you first.

Why not me?

The Dream Weaver

Nova sails across a bright tangerine sea.
Ze is beaming, irradiating joy.
Ze holds Bindi's hand. They are in love.
The water whispers words of encouragement.

"You are my galaxy," Nova says. "I know."
Bindi replies. Her cheeks are the softest shade of
pink, almost barely flushed.
Nova thinks in constellations. Speaks in stardust.
Bindi's green-gray eyes are dancing owl wings
in the moonlight.

Their world gives no life to secrets, only silence,
song, and spirit.
Soar… Angel eagles cry.

The lovers ride on waves of heartbeats and
blues, jazz....
sweet, low, and slow
Keeps the breath abreast
Feel the sax invested in your chest
Give into love's blessing, Pressing
On your reincarnated memory bank.

Jungle Man

my inner self is a jungle man
a beast that vine-swings like Tarzan

on the outside, i play mild
while my heart stays willfully wild,
never to be tamed or chained
living unseemly without any shame

Sunset

An invisible child resting on the crescent of Venus dips a few cumulus clouds in his mother's blush powder. Streaks of golden highlight begin to fade from earth's face. The boy wields the darkest purple mascara he can find across the stratosphere like a crayon. He does manage, however, to blend lilac eyeshadow on the moon's closed eyelid a bit more gracefully. His mother awakens as the first star does a scintillating pirouette. He giggles and scampers off to the sighs of a sleepy city.